Hidden Life

What's Living on Your Body?

Andrew Solway

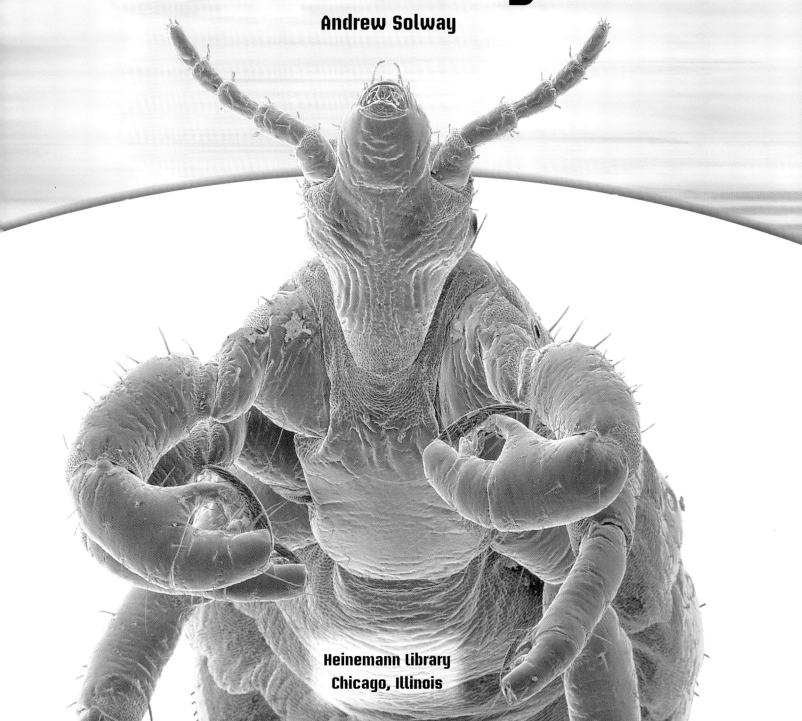

Heinemann Library
Chicago, Illinois

© 2004 Heinemann Library
a division of Reed Elsevier, Inc.
Chicago, Illinois

Customer Service 888-454-2279
Visit our website at www.heinemannlibrary.com

Designed by David Poole and Paul Myerscough
Illustrations by Geoff Ward
Originated by Dot Gradations
Printed and bound in China by South China Printing Company

08 07
10 9 8 7 6 5 4 3 2

          Library of Congress Cataloging-in-Publication Data
Solway, Andrew.
  What's living on your body? / Andrew Solway.
        v. cm. -- (Hidden life)
Includes bibliographical references and index.
Contents: Take a closer look -- Vampire insects -- Jumping fleas --
Hitch-hiking ticks -- Tiny mites -- Pollen up your nose -- Friendly
bacteria -- Microbes in your mouth -- Bacteria-hunters -- Microbe
problems -- Nosy viruses.
  ISBN 1-4034-4848-5 (HC library binding) -- ISBN 1-4034-5487-6 (PB)
  ISBN 978-1-4034-4848-4 (HC) -- ISBN 978-1-4034-5487-4 (PB)
  1. Body, Human--Microbiology--Juvenile literature. 2.
Insects--Juvenile literature. [1. Body, Human. 2. Microorganisms.] I.
Title. II. Series.
  QR171.A1S65 2004
  612--dc22
                        2003018002

Acknowledgments
The author and publishers are grateful to the following for permission to reproduce
copyright material: pp. 4a, 19b Tudor photography; Science Photo Library pp. 4b, 6, 10a, 11,
13a (Eye of Science), p. 5 (BSIP/Laurent), p. 7a (Dr Chris Hale), p. 7b, 8 (David Scharf), p. 9a
(K H Kjeldsen), p. 10b (Darwin Dale), p. 12a (Andrew Syred), p. 13b (Dr P Marazzi), p. 14
(Dr Jeremy Burgess), p. 15a (Eddy Gray), p. 15b (Damien Lovegrove), p. 16a (Dr Tony Brain),
p. 16b (Science Pictures Ltd) p. 17 (Dr Kari Lounatmaa), p. 18 (Dr Linda Stannard, UCT), p.
19a (Volker Steger), pp. 20a, 20b, 21 (Eric Grave), p. 23 (Biophoto Associates), p. 24 (Linda
Steinmark, Custom Medical Stock Photo), p. 26 (Richard T Nowitz), p.27 (CNRI);
Oxford Scientific Film p. 9b; Science Photo Library pp. 12b, 22, 25b.

Cover photograph of an itch mite reproduced with permission of Eye of Science/Science
Photo Library.

Our thanks to Dr. Philip Parrillo, entomologist at the Field Museum in Chicago, for his
comments in the preparation of this book.

Every effort has been made to contact copyright holders of any material reproduced in this
book. Any omissions will be rectified in subsequent printings if notice is given to the
publishers.

Some words are shown in bold, **like this.** You can find out
what they mean by looking in the glossary.

Contents

Many of the photos in this book were taken using a microscope.
In the captions you may see a number that tells you how much
they have been enlarged. For example, a photo marked "(x200)"
is about 200 times bigger than in real life.

Take a Closer Look

You probably think that you know your body really well. You have seen yourself many times in mirrors and in photos. You know how your body looks, feels, and smells. But if you move in close enough, you will see your body as a strange landscape, a world full of hidden microscopic life.

Imagine taking a good look around your body using a microscope. As you increase the magnification, you will find more and more examples of hidden life.

Getting up close

Look at your skin at low magnification. It is covered with a network of lines and

From a distance your skin looks smooth. But under a microscope, the tiny pores (holes) can be seen, as the photo on the right shows (x800). The pores lead to glands that produce sweat and oils.

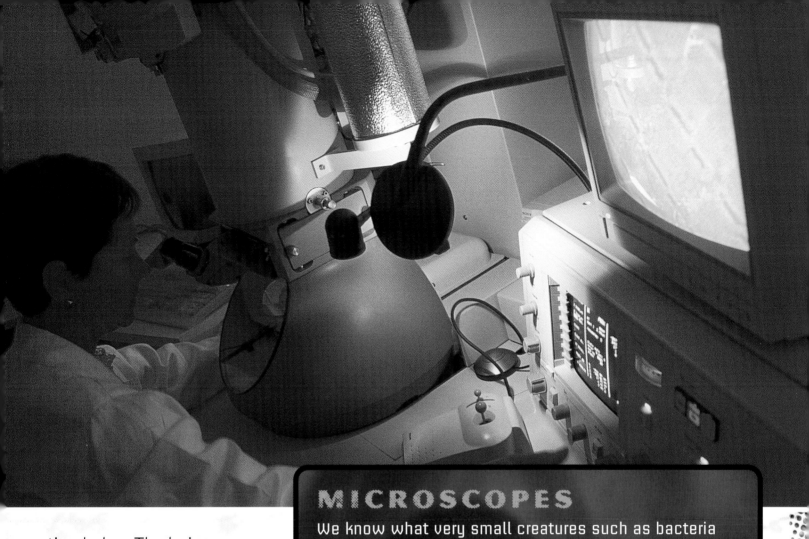

tiny holes. The hairs on your skin are like tree trunks, and the hair on your head is a forest. Tiny insects can live in this forest. Even tinier creatures can live on your eyelashes, eating bits of skin and oils that the skin produces.

Closer still

At high magnification, you will find that just about every part of your skin is home to microscopic creatures. Most are **bacteria**—simple living things made of only a

MICROSCOPES

We know what very small creatures such as bacteria and viruses look like because scientists have used microscopes to study them. A light microscope, the type of microscope you may have used yourself, can magnify up to about 1,800 times. But to look at really tiny things, scientists use **electron microscopes,** which can magnify objects up to 500,000 times.

single **cell.** We think of bacteria as germs that cause disease, but most of the ones that live on your skin are harmless.

Up your nose!

Now let's increase the power of your microscope to 100,000 times and look at some of the microscopic

life inside your nose! You will see some of the smallest living things of all—**viruses.** Outside of another living cell, viruses are just tiny packages of a few complex chemicals. But if they get inside a cell, they can make thousands of copies of themselves and cause illness in the process.

Vampire Insects

Have you ever had an itchy head that bothered you for days? If so, you might have had an attack of head lice. We might call these annoying pests vampire insects because of their bloodsucking ways. Luckily they usually cause nothing worse than itching.

Grains of lice

Lice are **parasites,** which means that they live and feed on their human **host.** Adult lice are grayish-white insects the size of a grain of rice. They have no wings, and their bodies are flattened. They use their strong, hooklike claws to hang onto hair. Lice live for about a month, but they cannot survive for more than about two days if they are off their host.

This is a human head louse (x150).

Feeding

Lice's mouthparts are designed for sucking blood. A set of curved hooks around the mouth dig into the skin when the louse is about to eat. Then two thin tubes pierce the skin. The louse's saliva helps the tubes go in and prevents the blood from **clotting.**

Lice eat two or three times a day. After a meal, a louse looks reddish brown because of the blood inside it.

Louse eggs

Louse eggs are called **nits.** Females "superglue" nits to hairs, which makes them hard to remove. The nits take eight or nine days to hatch.

Growing up

When they hatch, young lice look similar to adults. They are known as **nymphs.** The nymphs begin to eat blood almost as soon as they hatch. They grow quickly, and after about nine days are mature adults.

This photo shows nits in a girl's hair. The egg case has a lid that pops open when the louse hatches.

This is a human body louse. Body lice look similar to head lice, but they only appear when people are living in cramped, dirty conditions.

GETTING RID OF LICE

Head lice do not mind clean hair, and they often get passed from person to person at school. If you do get lice, there are many ways to get rid of them. Lice do not like oil, so oiling your hair and combing it can get rid of them. There are also special shampoos that you can use.

Jumping Fleas

Head lice live in hair, but we can also get unwanted guests on our bodies. Fleas are tiny wingless insects about 0.08 inch (2 mm) long. They hop onto us to grab a meal of blood and then jump off again.

Fleas on the wrong host

Fleas are **parasites** that spend some of their time in the **host's** bedding and only get on the host to feed. Different kinds of fleas feed on different animals. The fleas that most often bite people are cat or dog fleas that jump onto a human by mistake. They take a quick meal, but human blood is not to their taste so they hop off again.

There is another kind of flea that lives mainly on humans. But they only like dirty clothes and bedding, so you can avoid them by washing regularly.

What do fleas look like?

A flea's body is very narrow, which makes it easy for fleas to move through fur. Fleas have pointed mouthparts that they use to pierce their host's skin and suck up blood.

A flea's body is covered in backward-pointing bristles. It can move forward smoothly, but if it moves backward the bristles cling to the host's fur, anchoring the flea in place.

Leaping tall buildings

Fleas get on and off their hosts by jumping, and they have an astonishing jump. A flea can jump up to 100 times its body length. If you could do that, you would be able to jump over a 40-story skyscraper!

Fleas use more than just muscle power to jump. When a flea bends its back legs before a jump, the bending motion **compresses** a thick pad of springy material at the top of the leg. When this pad is released, it suddenly springs back into shape, giving the flea a tremendous boost of power.

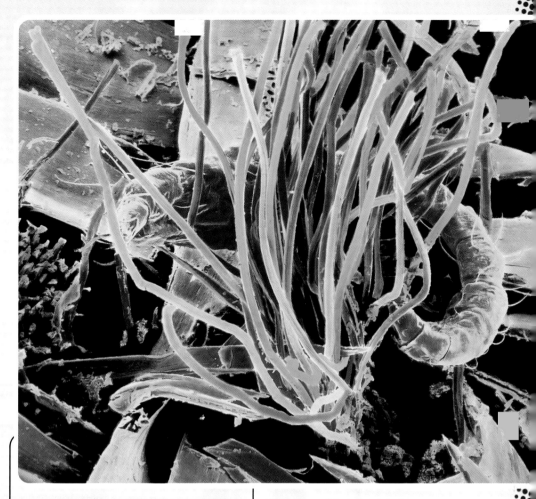

This flea larva (yellow) is coiled around fibers in a carpet. Flea larvae are blind and wormlike.

Flea lives

Female fleas lay their eggs in the nest or den of their host. In the case of dog or cat fleas, this means in your pet's bed. Young fleas **(larvae)** take a week or more to develop. Then they spin a silken **cocoon.** About a week later, an adult flea breaks out from the cocoon.

The most likely way for fleas to get onto your body is from your pets. So if your dog or cat is scratching a lot, check for fleas.

Hitchhiking Ticks

Like fleas, ticks hitch rides on humans and take a blood meal as they ride along. Certain kinds of ticks can carry serious diseases.

Ticks are not insects, but eight-legged relatives of spiders. Several kinds of ticks feed on humans.

A meal a year

At each stage in their lives, ticks eat only one large blood meal and then drop off their **host.** Ticks go through three main stages in their lives—larvae, **nymphs,** and adults. Each stage can take a year or more. So in three years a tick gets three meals at most. Males miss out on the last meal, so they get only two.

Adult deer ticks are smaller than a pinhead. This one has been magnified 25 times. Deer ticks can carry an illness called Lyme disease.

From eggs to larvae

Female ticks lay several thousand eggs. The **larvae** that hatch from the eggs have only six legs. To eat, a larva needs to find a host. So it climbs a grass stalk or other plant and waits for a host animal to brush past.

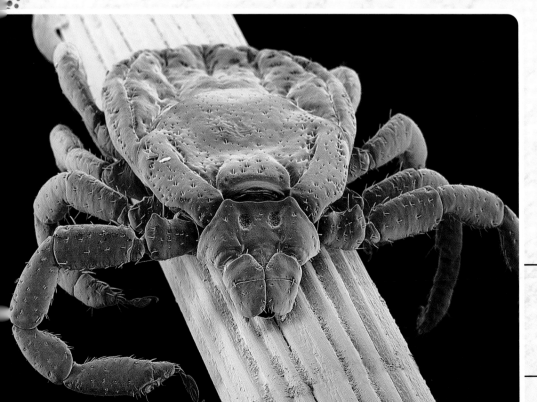

*Dog ticks can pass **bacteria** that cause a serious disease called typhus. This dog tick is enlarged 45 times.*

If the right kind of animal comes by, the tick crawls on and takes a meal. Once it has eaten, the tick drops off the host and then **molts** to become a nymph.

From nymph to adult

Tick nymphs have eight legs. Like the larvae, nymphs look for a host, take a meal, and then drop off. Some kinds of ticks feed on the same kind of host animal as before, while others feed on a different kind of host.

After its second meal, the tick drops off and molts once again to become an adult. The adults mate, and male ticks die soon afterward. Females take a last meal and then lay their eggs.

Ticks and disease

Usually, a tick will cause nothing worse than a sore, itchy bite. But some types of ticks can carry disease. In the United States, for instance, tiny deer ticks

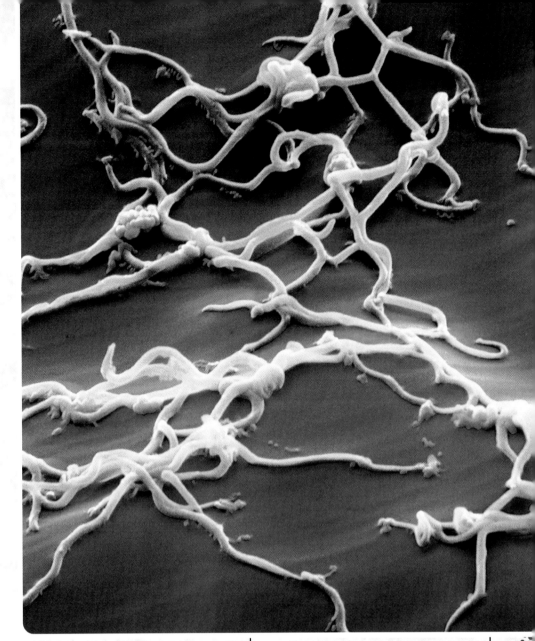

can cause Lyme disease. This diseases causes a rash and flulike symptoms followed by painful, swollen joints.

*Ticks do not cause disease, but they can be infected with harmful **microbes** and pass them on to their **host.** These stringy-looking bacteria (x9560) cause Lyme disease in humans.*

BIG APPETITES

In one meal, a tick can suck up as much as 100 times its own weight in blood. As it feeds, it pumps most of the water from the blood back into its host. If it didn't do this, it would burst.

Tiny Mites

Although lice, fleas, and ticks are small, you soon notice if they bite you. Eyelash mites do not bite, and they are so tiny that you may never know they are there. But their relatives, the itch mites, are not so easy to live with.

Like ticks, mites are relatives of spiders and have eight legs. But not all mites are **parasites** or bloodsuckers.

Mites on your eyelashes

Eyelash mites, or follicle mites, are tiny creatures that live on the face, particularly around the eyelashes and ears. They live near **hair follicles** and feed on skin and on oils produced by the follicles.

Even the cleanest people can get follicle mites. Most of us have them at some time in our lives. They usually cause no harm, but doctors think that they sometimes help cause acne (pimples) on the faces of teenagers.

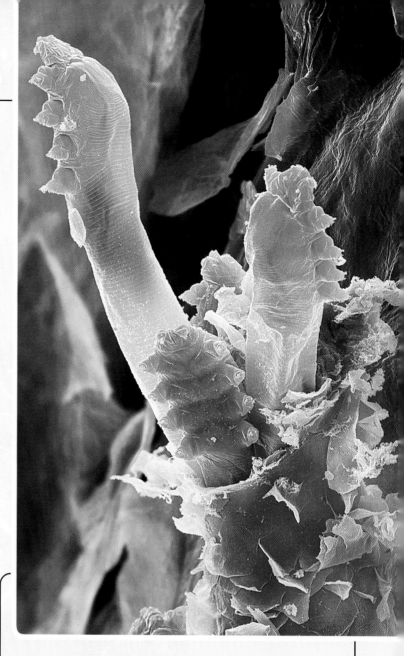

This follicle shows mites (x390) sticking out of a hair follicle. These mites are about 0.004 inch (0.1 mm) long. The front part of the body (seen here) has four pairs of short, stubby legs.

Itch mites

Itch mites are much more unpleasant than follicle mites. They cause a rash called scabies. Luckily they are much less common, too, so you are unlikely to get them unless you come into contact with an infected person.

Itch mites are about the same size as follicle mites and, like follicle mites, they eat human skin. They would be fairly harmless except that when female mites have mated, they dig tunnels into the skin to lay their eggs. These tunnels cause terrible itching. Constant scratching can cause wounds that may become infected.

Female itch mites tunnel into the skin, mainly on the hands and wrists, and lay two or three eggs each day. The tunnels can be 1.2 inches (3 cm) deep and cause severe itching.

MITES ARE EVERYWHERE!

Mites are not very big, but they are very successful. There are more than 40,000 kinds of mites, and they are found just about everywhere. Mites live on animals and plants, in the soil, in rivers and lakes, and deep in the ocean. Some mites live in hot springs, at temperatures of up to 122 °F (50 °C), while other mites in Antarctica can survive at -112 °F (-80 °C).

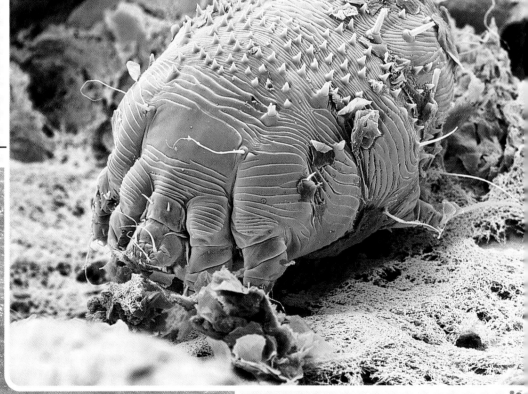

Itch mite tunnels cause wounds and scratching that then create blisters, scabs, and a red rash known as scabies. Scabies can be passed on by close contact with an infected person.

Pollen Up Your Nose

Every spring and summer, the air is filled with clouds of fine, yellow dust called **pollen.** Most pollen comes from flowers. Each flower produces clouds of pollen, some of which will reach another flower of the same kind and **fertilize** it. But the rest of the pollen gets everywhere—in your hair, on your clothes, and up your nose.

A cloud of pollen is released by Alnus cordata *catkins.*

Pollen grains are not living creatures, but they contain a germ of life inside them. They are the male **sex cells** of flowering plants—like the **sperm** of male animals. When a grain of pollen meets up with an egg cell from a flower of the same kind, the two join together. From this joined cell come the seeds that will grow into new plants.

Amazing shapes

Pollen grains are tiny. To our eyes they look like very fine dust. But if you put pollen grains under the microscope, you find that they are not simply small, round balls. The hard outer casing of each grain is a marvelously sculpted shape.

Pollen grains from different plants look very different. Some have spikes all over their surface, which help them to stick to animals or insects. Pollen that is designed to be carried by insects is usually larger than pollen that relies on the wind to carry it to the female flower.

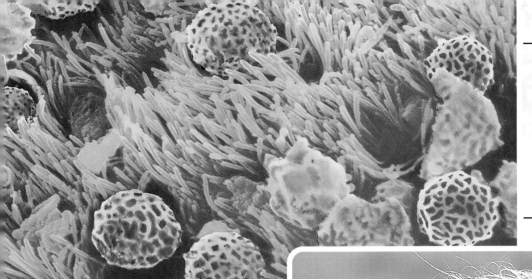

Pollen on people

At times of the year when there is a lot of pollen in the air, you breathe in pollen grains every time you go outside. The pollen grains get trapped in the sticky mucus that lines your nose and throat. In many people, this pollen does no harm, but some people are **allergic** to it. Their bodies act as if the pollen grains are invading germs, and the result is hay fever. It causes a stuffy nose, sneezing, and red, watery eyes. Pollen is also thought to make **asthma** worse.

Not all types of pollen cause allergies. Only small pollen grains are light enough to be carried far by the wind. Also, chemicals on the outside of the pollen affect whether it causes allergies or not.

People who suffer from hay fever start sneezing if they go outside when there is a lot of pollen in the air.

LONG-DISTANCE TRAVELERS

Pollen grains from ragweed flowers are long-distance travelers. They have been found 400 miles (650 km) out to sea and 2 miles (3 km) up in the air.

Friendly Bacteria

Did you know that your skin is crawling with **microbes?** It is not because you are dirty. Washing will not get rid of them all. These microbes are not dangerous germs, but harmless residents that actually help keep us healthy.

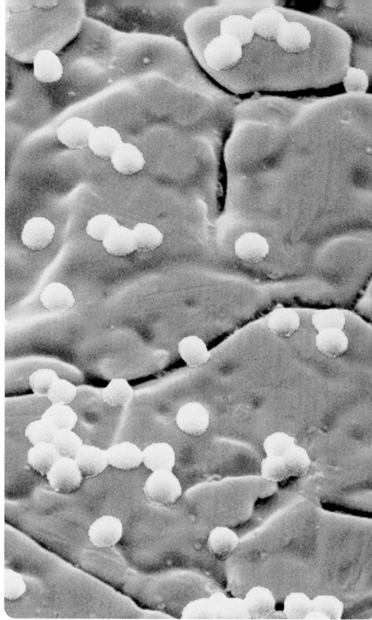

Skin infections can be caused by the bacteria Staphylococcus aureus, which often grow in clusters of small spheres (x8530).

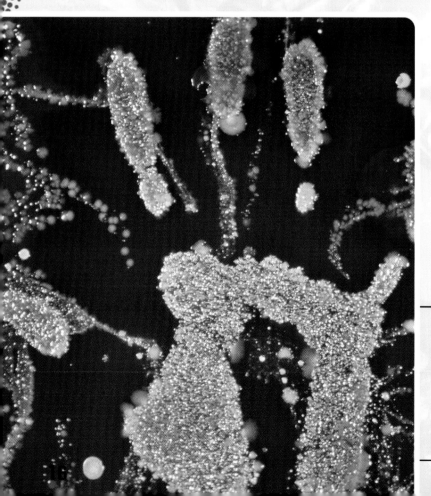

About 50 different kinds of microbes live on our skin, and most of them are **bacteria.** Some bacteria, called bacilli, are rod-shaped. Others, called cocci, are round or oval, and a few kinds, called spirilli, are spiral. The rods and spirals often have whiplike tails called flagella.

This photo shows a "bacterial handprint." A hand was pressed onto a plate of agar gel, leaving behind some of the bacteria that were on the hand. The gel contained food for the bacteria, and after a time, large colonies of bacteria grew in the shape of the handprint.

Favorite places

Bacteria live all over your body, even on your eyes. In some places there are billions, and in others only a few. To a bacterium, our bodies are enormous. They seem as big as a whole planet. Warm, moist places such as armpits and between the toes, for instance, are good places for bacteria to live. Those places may be home to billions of bacteria. Other parts of the body have no microbes. The arms and legs have only several thousand bacteria per square inch (6 cm^2).

Protective microbes

The bacteria best adapted to living on our skin cause us no harm. In fact, they help protect us by eating food and taking up living space that might otherwise be used by disease-causing bacteria. Scientists have found that if an animal is brought up with no microbes on its skin, as few as ten harmful bacteria can make the animal ill, whereas it would take about a million bacteria to infect a normal animal.

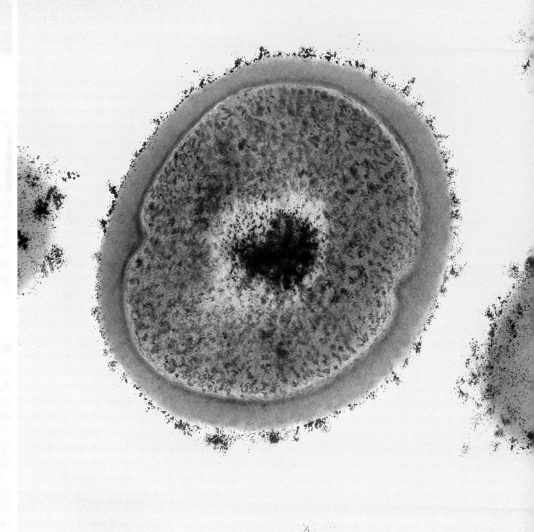

Staphylococcus aureus *bacteria, like this one (x200,980), are common on the skin.*

STINKY SWEAT

Sweaty bodies can get very smelly. For proof, just go into a locker room after a game. But sweat is simply salty water produced by special sweat **glands** in the skin. It does not smell. The odor comes from the waste products of billions of bacteria and other microbes living around your sweat glands.

Microbes in Your Mouth

There may be billions of **microbes** on your skin, but there are many more in your mouth. Your mouth is a wonderful place for **bacteria** to grow. It is warm and moist, and a feast of food passes through it every day.

Over 200 kinds of microbes live on the skin, but there are almost 80 different types in the mouth alone. As on the skin, they take up space that could otherwise be occupied by harmful microbes.

Although the mouth is moist and there is plenty of food, the microbes do not take over or cause harm. Every time you eat, you swallow millions of them, and they are killed by the strong acid in your stomach. Your saliva (spit) also contains natural **antibiotics.**

*Spiral bacteria (Spirochetes) like these are common in the mouth. Unlike other types of bacteria, Spirochetes do not have a hard outer **cell** wall.*

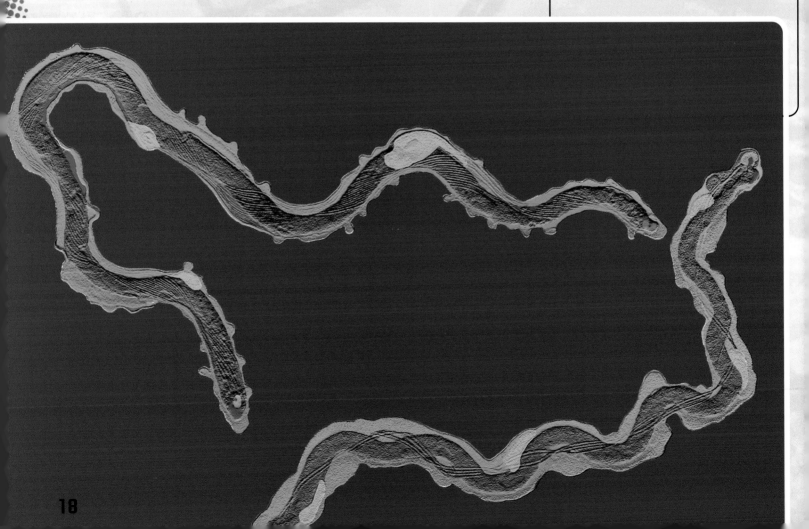

Between the teeth

A favorite place for bacteria and other microbes is the gaps between the teeth and the places where the teeth meet the gums.

A thin film several hundred microbes thick can build up in these places. This film is called **plaque.** Many kinds of bacteria grow in plaque, including *Spirochetes*, which are not found on the skin. Some **yeasts,** which are a kind of **fungus,** also grow there.

This tooth has been cut through and photographed in special light to show decay.

Tooth decay

Some of the microbes in plaque do no harm. But some bacteria, in particular those called *Streptococcus mutans,* cause problems. They feed on the sugars in food and produce acid as a waste product. This acid can damage the hard outer covering of your teeth, called enamel. Eventually a hole may be worn in the tooth, and bacteria can get in and cause tooth decay.

Brushing your teeth regularly stops the buildup of bacteria and helps prevent tooth decay.

Bacteria Hunters

Bacteria are not the only **microbes** living in the mouth. Some bacteria-eating microbes also live there. These bacteria hunters are called **amoebas.** They help keep down the number of bacteria in the mouth.

Amoebas are more complicated than bacteria. Their **cells** are like the cells that make up larger animals, not like bacterial cells. In particular, they have a **nucleus,** while bacteria do not.

Getting around

The outside of the amoeba is a thin, bendable membrane, or skin. The material inside the membrane is called cytoplasm. Amoebas' cytoplasm can change easily from a liquid to a jellylike solid. This is important for the way the amoeba moves around.

To move forward, the amoeba pushes out fingerlike parts of the cytoplasm called **pseudopods.**

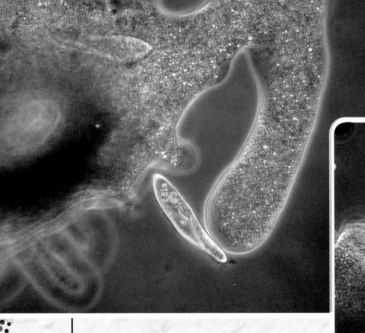

In the photo above, an amoeba is about to surround a microbe (bottom right of the photo). In the photo on the right, the microbe is inside the amoeba.

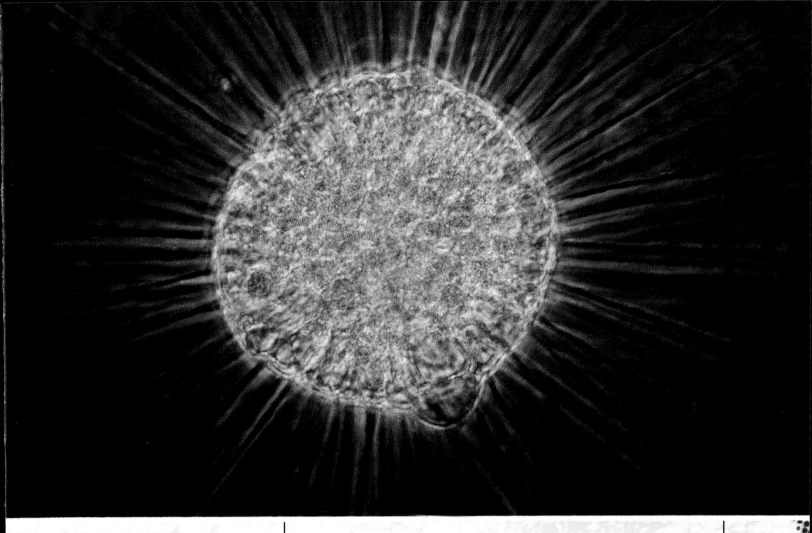

Catching bacteria

Amoebas also catch bacteria with their pseudopods. They reach out with long pseudopods to surround their prey without touching it. Then the pseudopods close in, until the prey is trapped in a small, round, baglike **vacuole.** The amoeba then digests the prey and absorbs its **nutrients.**

Types of amoeba

The amoebas that live in the mouth are part of a group called *Entamoeba.*

◑ *The kind of pseudopod an amoeba makes can help to identify it. This amoeba,* Actinosphaerium eichhorni, *has thin, spiky pseudopods.*

Some others in this group live in the stomach and can cause ulcers. Amoebas can also live in the ocean, in fresh water, and in the soil.

Most are microscopic, but some can be up to 0.2 inch (5 mm) long. These giant amoebas have many nuclei, rather than just one.

AMOEBA RELATIVES

Amoebas are part of a large, loose grouping of one-celled creatures called **protozoans.** Protozoans generally need to eat food to survive, like animals, while **algae** can make their own food as plants do. Not very many kinds of protozoans live on the body, but some can cause diseases if they get through the skin.

Microbe Problems

Most of the time we do not notice the billions of **microbes** on our skin. But sometimes something goes wrong. **Bacteria** get through the skin's defenses and cause problems, or microbes that do not usually live on the skin move in and take over.

Boiling up

Many bacteria live inside a **hair follicle** rather than on the skin surface. The follicle is a pit in the skin containing the hair root and an oil-producing **gland** called the **sebaceous gland.** The oil from the sebaceous gland keeps the hair from getting dry and brittle.

Normally dead **cells** and bacteria from the hair follicle are carried to the skin surface by this oil. But sometimes a mixture of oil and dead cells clogs up the top of the hair follicle, and it fills up with oil and cells. Bacteria also build up in the follicle, and chemicals they produce cause irritation and swelling. The result is a pimple.

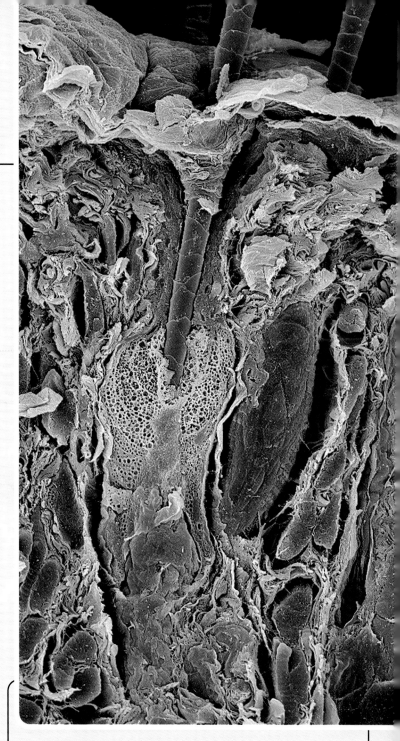

This photo of a hair follicle (x295) shows the hair (brown), the hair root (green), and the sebaceous gland (the blue structure to the right of the hair root).

Everyone occasionally gets a pimple or two. However, teenagers often get many bad ones, known as acne. This is because during the teenage years our sebaceous glands produce more oil.

Fungi on your feet

Another part of the skin where microbes can cause problems is the feet. Feet are warm and damp, which are good conditions for bacteria. The bacteria do not do anything worse than make your feet smell, although smelly feet can be pretty bad! But if your feet are hot and sweaty a lot, the conditions become ideal for the growth of some kinds of **fungi.** They cause a skin disease called athlete's foot.

Athlete's foot gets its name because the disease is usually spread in places such as swimming pools and locker rooms. It starts as dry, itchy skin between the toes. The skin then cracks, and blisters may form. If it is not treated, the disease may spread to other parts of the body.

Athlete's foot is caused by a group of fungi called dermatophytes. These fungi (shown here in orange) are made up of microscopic branching threads that cover the skin cells (in blue and yellow).

Nosy Viruses

The very smallest **microbes** that live on your body are **viruses.** Viruses are incredibly tiny—they can be 100 times smaller than **bacteria.** The best place to look for these teeny microbes is up your nose.

Many different viruses live on the inside of your nose and in your throat. Like the bacteria that live on us, most are harmless. But if we get some kinds of viruses in our nose, we get a cold.

Getting a cold

We get colds by breathing cold viruses in from the air or by touching a surface with viruses on it and then touching our noses. Colds are not caused by one type of virus. There are over 100 different cold viruses.

When you sneeze, stuff shoots out from your nose at over 100 miles per hour (160 kmph).

How a virus works

When a cold virus lands on the inside of your nose, it gets into a cell of the nose lining. Once inside the cell, it takes control. Instead of doing its normal job, the cell starts churning out hundreds of copies of the virus. Eventually it becomes so full that it bursts open, releasing the virus copies to infect other cells.

It takes eight to twelve hours from the time a cold virus enters the nose to the release of the first wave of viral copies. This is when the first cold symptoms begin to show up.

Sneezing and coughing

A cold infection usually affects only a small part of the nose because our body's defenses react quickly and many of the viruses are killed. But the body also defends itself against the virus by causing sneezing and coughing, to get the viruses out of the body. So most of the effects of a cold are caused by the body itself.

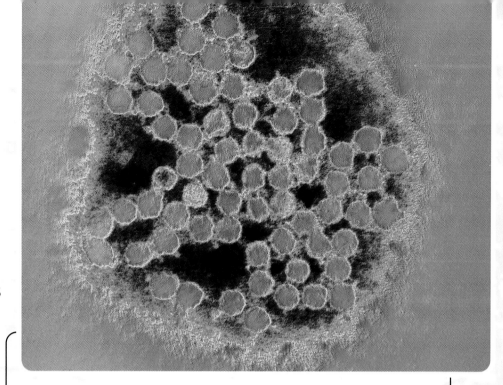

The rhinovirus is one of the causes of the common cold. Here it has been magnified 219,600 times.

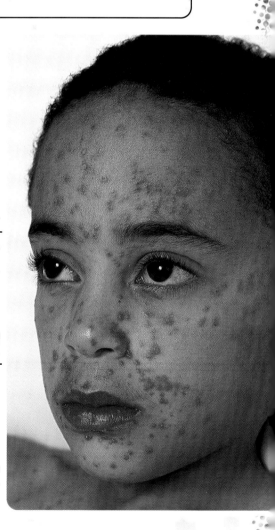

Chicken pox is another disease caused by viruses. As with colds and flu, the virus can be passed on when a person with chicken pox sneezes or coughs.

NOT ONLY COLDS

Colds are not the only illnesses caused by viruses. Flu, measles, chicken pox, smallpox, and bronchitis are just some of the many other viral diseases. As with colds and flu, the viruses for measles, chicken pox, and bronchitis can be spread through the air

Barrier Breakers

The skin is the first line of the body's defenses against disease. It is hard for **microbes** to get through its many layers. But some microbes have found a way around this defense. They get themselves injected straight into the bloodstream.

A tough barrier to cross

Your skin is an excellent barrier to microbes. The top layers of the skin are made up of flattened, dead **cells** full of a tough substance called **keratin.**

Among mosquitoes, only the females carry disease. Their needlelike mouthparts easily pierce human skin. Males have different mouthparts and feed only on nectar.

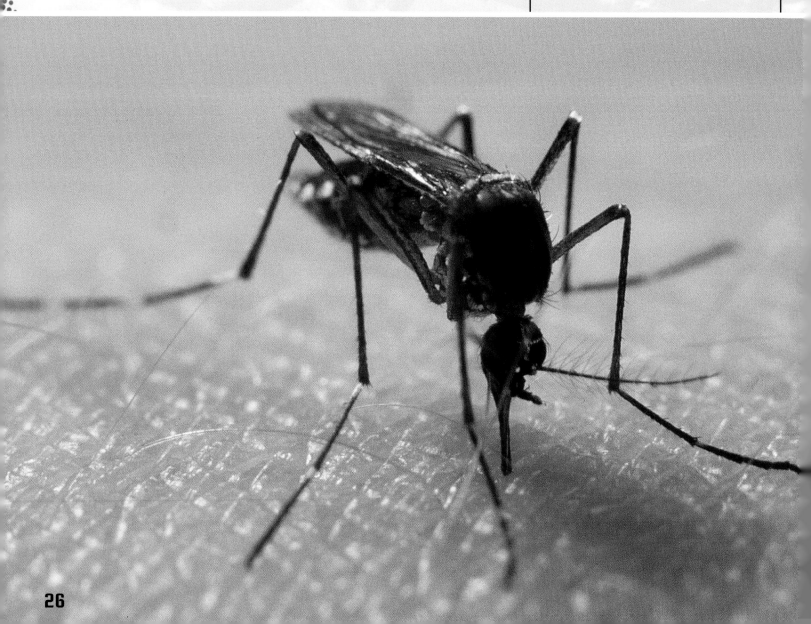

Hard protection

Keratin is the same substance that makes up your nails and the horns of many animals (in nails and horns the keratin is much thicker). The cells are glued together by a kind of cement, and oils from the **sebaceous glands** make the skin waterproof. A bacterium, which is less than a tenth the size of a single cell, has a hard time getting through this tough barrier.

Getting past the skin

One way that microbes get past this obstacle is through an insect bite. Some of the bloodsuckers we have described, in particular ticks, can carry disease-causing microbes. They pick up these microbes by feeding on an animal infected with them.

Deer ticks, for instance, pick up the **bacteria** that cause Lyme disease from infected mice. If an infected tick then bites a human, the tick passes the bacteria into the person's blood.

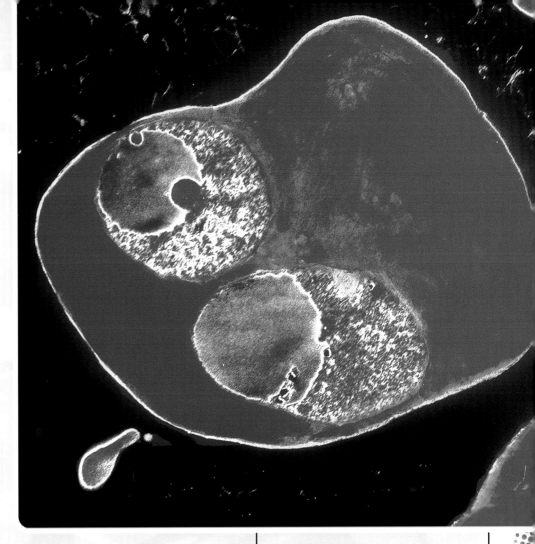

Mosquito carrier

Probably the top disease-carrying insect is the mosquito. It can carry many different diseases, including malaria.

Malaria is caused not by a bacterium but by a **protozoan** called *Plasmodium.* When an infected mosquito feeds on a human, it injects saliva into the bloodstream to stop the blood from **clotting.** The *Plasmodium* gets into the blood in this saliva.

This red blood cell (x17,650) is from someone with malaria. It has two Plasmodium protozoans inside it. Eventually the blood cell will burst.

In humans, *Plasmodium* acts kind of like a **virus,** getting into blood cells and reproducing inside them until the cells burst. If a mosquito feeds on a person who has malaria, it sucks up some *Plasmodium* with its blood meal. Then the whole cycle can begin again.

Table of Sizes

Although all hidden life is tiny, there is a huge range of sizes. To a flea, a grain of pollen seems just as tiny as the flea seems to us.

Dog tick
5 – 6 mm

Deer tick
3 – 4 mm

Head louse
0.7 mm

Plasmodium
0.1 – 0.3 mm

Follicle mite
200 µm

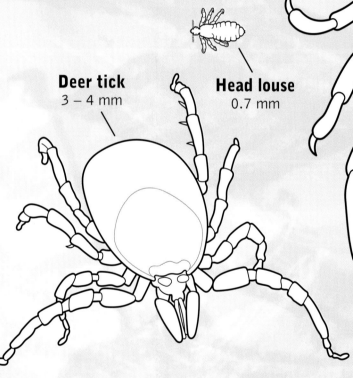

These organisms are 20 times bigger than normal.

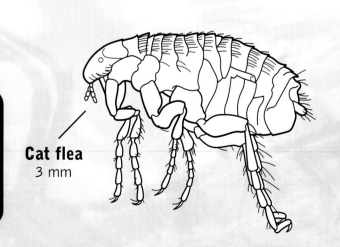

Cat flea
3 mm

HOW SMALL?

1 m (meter) = 1,000 mm (millimeters)
1 mm (millimeter) = 1,000 µm (micrometers)
1 µm (micrometer) = 1,000 nm (nanometers)

28

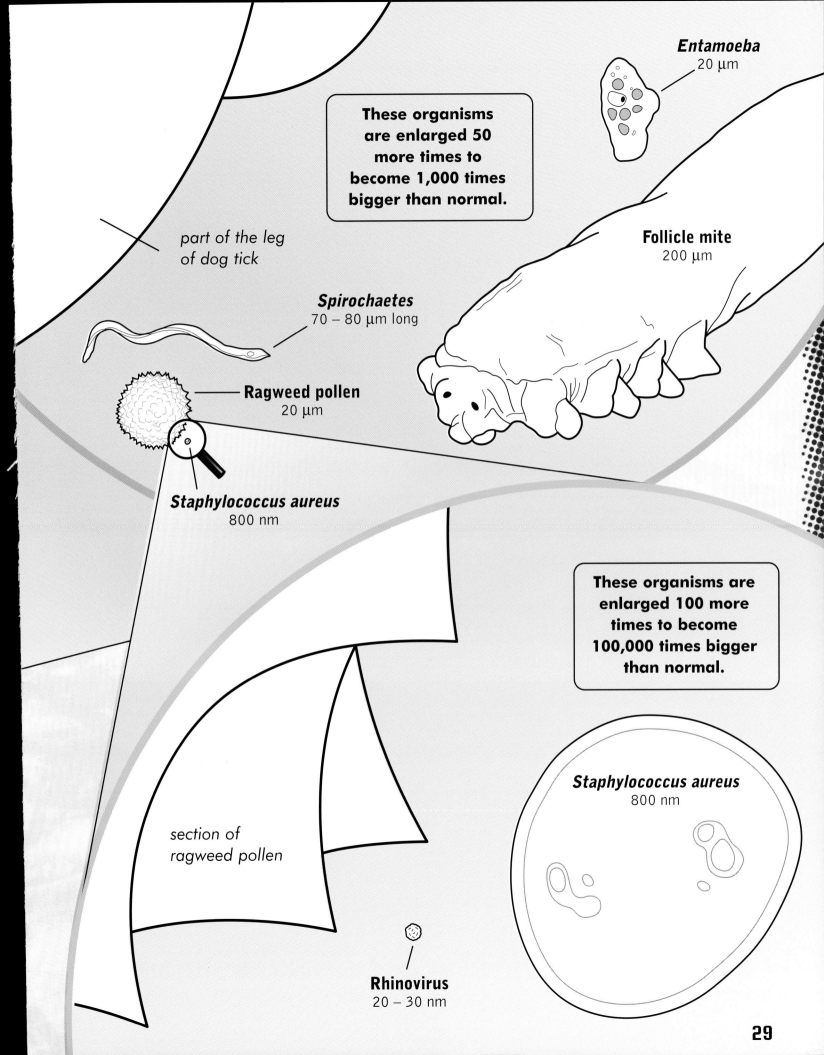

Entamoeba
20 µm

These organisms are enlarged 50 more times to become 1,000 times bigger than normal.

part of the leg of dog tick

Follicle mite
200 µm

Spirochaetes
70 – 80 µm long

Ragweed pollen
20 µm

Staphylococcus aureus
800 nm

These organisms are enlarged 100 more times to become 100,000 times bigger than normal.

section of ragweed pollen

Staphylococcus aureus
800 nm

Rhinovirus
20 – 30 nm

Glossary

algae   members of large group of plantlike creatures, most of which are microscopic

allergy/allergic   condition in which the body overreacts to something that is breathed in, eaten, or gets on the skin. It can cause sneezing, rash, or sickness.

amoeba   one-celled microbes that move and catch food by sending out fingerlike structures called pseudopods

antibiotic   drug or natural chemical that kills bacteria or stops them from growing

asthma   disease of the lungs that causes wheezing and other breathing difficulties

bacteria   microscopic creatures, each one only a single cell. They are different from other one-celled creatures because they do not have a nucleus. Only one of these living things is called a bacterium.

cells   building blocks of living things. Some living things are single cells, while others are made up of billions of cells working together.

clotting   formation of a solid clump of blood caused by special substances in the blood. Clotting stops a wound from bleeding.

cocoon   silky, cigar-shaped case spun by many species of insect larvae to protect themselves while they change from larvae into adults

compress   squash into less space

electron microscope   very powerful microscope that can magnify objects up to 500,000 times

enamel   hard outer coating of the teeth

fertilize   to form a new plant or animal by joining a male sex cell, called a sperm, with a female sex cell, called an egg

fungus   plantlike living thing such as a mushroom or a yeast. Two or more of these organisms are called fungi.

gland   organ in the body that produces a chemical or other substance

hair follicle   small hole or pit in the skin that contains the root of the hair and the sebaceous gland

host   animal or plant on which a parasite lives

keratin   tough substance that makes up nails, horns, hair, and skin

larva   young stage of some types of insects. A larva looks different from an adult and has to go through a changing stage (the pupa) in order to become an adult.

microbe   microscopic creature such as a bacterium, protozoan, or virus

molt   to shed hair, feathers, or skin

nits   eggs and egg cases of lice

nucleus   round structure surrounded by a membrane found inside a living cell. It contains the cell's genes.

nutrient   chemical that nourishes living things

nymph   young of some types of insects and mites. Nymphs usually look similar to their parents and change gradually into adults during several molts.

parasite   creature that lives on or in another living creature and takes its food, without giving any benefit in return and sometimes causing harm

plaque   thin film, rich in bacteria, that forms on the teeth

pollen   fine powder produced by flowers to fertilize other flowers

protein   important substance that is used to build structures within living things and to control the thousands of chemical reactions that happen inside cells

protozoan   one-celled creature that is larger and more complicated than a bacterium

pseudopod   fingerlike structure that an amoeba sends out in order to move around and to capture food. The word means "false foot."

sebaceous gland   oil-producing gland in a hair follicle

sex cell   special cell produced by female and male living things in order to reproduce. If the male and female sex cells combine, a new life is formed.

sperm   male sex cells of humans and many other animals

vacuole   fluid-filled bag inside a cell

virus   very tiny microbe that has to infect a living cell in order to grow or reproduce

yeast   microscopic one-celled fungus

More Books to Read

Grolier Educational Staff. *Around People: Friends, Pests, Parasites, and Freeloaders.* Danbury, Conn.: Scholastic Library Publishing, 1999.

Hirschmann, Kris. *Ticks.* Farmington Hills, Mich.: Gale Group, 2004.

Walker, Richard. *Human Body Lab.* San Diego, Calif.: Silver Dolphin Books, 2003.

Woodward, John. *Pesky Parasites.* Chicago: Heinemann Library, 2003.

Woog, Adam. *The Microscope.* Farmington Hills, Mich.: Gale Group, 2004.

Index